UM STILLA THINKUN

by
Tina Chamberlain

PILCHARDS FOR TEA

I remember our Sunday night tea.
Our salad bowl filled ta the brim
all freshly prepared
then the pilchards appeared
they made ut quite crunchy n grim.

The red can come out n wus opened
mum ud bring ut n out they would tip.
They'd land on the plate
them ole bones I did hate
but the juice made a bloomun good dip.

We hed bread thut wus buttered n ready
mum ud cut ut all lovingly so.
Our salad in spring
wus a wonderful thing
all home grown n tasted just so.

But them pilchards well they were a rummun
I felt sorry fa them in thut tin.
I wus glad when I'd et um
ull never forget um
an I don't want a pilchard agin.

CARDS AROUND THE TABLE

The Sunday tea things cleared away
n whenever we were earble
we'd git our pennies out
ta play cards around the tearble.

We'd all sit there so patiently
our chairs formed in a ring
We'd put a penny in the middle
an another on a king.

The seven a diamonds made the start
then six or eight fill in
if ya dint hev them or another card
you'd put a penny in agin.

The object wus ta go around
an each one add a card
You'd go up or down ta form the suit
an sometimes thut wus hard.

There'd be six on us ta play the game
an at times thut got intense.
Especially if a king wus left
thut could hold twenty pence.

We'd all hev such a laugh
thus the way we used ta be.
An whoever lorst the game
ud hetta mearke the cuppa tea.

SUET PUDDUN N TREACLE

In the winter arter dinner
with ya fust course cleared n done,
when thus cold n wet outside
with no chance ta see the sun.

There's nothun like a pan wi water
with a bearsun in ta steam,
an inside a Suet Puddun
thus the afters of my dreams.

Just the smell when thut start cookun
make me feel all good inside,
then ya tip the bearsun on a plearte
an out the puddun slide.

Then wi a great old tin o treacle
thus tipped all over the top,
an blast me thut smelt lovely
none on us will leave a drop.

Me ole belly ull be stretchun
but ta leave ut seemed a sin
I kep a gorn till thus orl finished
An I can't git no more in.

QUOTE!!

<u>WHAT MA MUM SAID</u>

One day I asked my mum, "why when you go shoppun, do you allus buy an extra bag a sugar, n put ut in a jar in the pantry"?

To which my mum replied,
"well thus so ire got some if I run out".

Strange though thut may seem, I now do the same.

Oh! N I hint run out yet either

FROM MY WINDOW

From my window I saw rabbits
I saw birds a pickun seeds.
A little mouse go hidun
amongst the grown up weeds.

A Pheasant runnun quickly
just heard a sound I spose.
A little squirrel eatun nuts
Thas held atwin its toes.

A tractor in the distance
just see a silhouette
must be the farmer ploughun
Cos thut int the harvest yet.

The fields go on forever
just broken by the hedges
they make a frame around the crops
so you can see the edges.

The trees all green n leafy.
The spring is in the air.
I love ta watch the country life
at this lovely time a year.

KIDS N CONKERS

Lookun back through years of fun
at the things we used ta do.
I liked just playun Conkers
an I played wi one or two.

Mum would soak ma conkers
in vinegar over night
then heat em in the oven
till they were hard n right.

She would then find an ole shoelearce
an in the conker put a hole
tie the shoelearce through the middle
an I'd tearke ut orf ta school.

We'd play conkers in the playground
till our little hearts content.
I mighta rapped ma knuckles
but the conker never bent.

We used ta call thut fun ya see
an thut dint corst us a penny.
An our conker fights are still today
remembered by so many.

THE PHOTO OF MY PAST

Outside the road was quiet and still
Through the trees the sun shine bright
So obviously the springtime
though the photos black n white.

There's me an ma brother Clive.
Near him I look sa small
an um runnun away an in ma hands
thut look like our football.

Um laughun as he's chasin me
oh what a lovely scene
wi his trousers half way up his legs
he look so long n lean.

Oh then there's me there wi ma coat
wi the hem above ma knees
an the buttons done up ta ma chin
an um runnun in the breeze.

Ma hair thus all dishevelled.
Ma dignity thus gone,
an when ya look down at ma feet
ire got ma slippers on.

Fond memories they come to mind
in pictures they can last.
I love ta reminisce and smile
at the photo of my past.

WHEN I JUMPED OUTER THE WINDOW

Blast I gotta tellun orf
for what I cant remember
but I know thut wus a wet day
Probably near November.

We all lived in a bungalow
an Mother laid the law
N she put me in ma bedroom
an said she'd bolt the door.

Well as you ken imagine
i wus none too pleased wi that
i got ma coat orf a the door knob
an I found ma bobble hat.

I got up on the little stool
climbed on the window sill
an opened up the window
so thut wus wide enough until,

I could get ma little body through
I looked down towards the grass
I put ma best foot forward,
Jumped and landed on ma ..bottom.

I ran around the Bungalow
an near the window mum stood cookun
she saw me tear orf round the path
I dint think she'd be a lookun.

I ran so fast towards the lane
an with har rollun pin
Mother tore outa the kitchen
an was arter me agin.

I ran up the leafy lane
I'd left home, I was gone
But I heard ma mum a shoutun,
"Gal you're got ya slippers on"

I ran round to Mrs. Barkers
who I'd always go n see
an I told har I'd left home
an she laughed out loud ta me.

She said, "come n hev a biscuit,
pick a nice one from the jar,
then you'll have to go back home
Cos mum ull wonder where ya are".

So I hed ma little biscuit
an back down the lane I went
Mum knew all along
Thut back home I'd soon be sent.

She saw me comun round the door
I wanted just to hugger
She say," gorn out like that wi slippers on
You silly little ....sod."

I really felt defeated
I wanted just to cry
But mum brought me through
a lovely dish wi home made apple pie.

ON THE BIKE SEAT

My journey ta the fust school.
A sight fa all ta see.
Mum hed a bike
with a seat I dint like
all metal an carried ole me.

I wus positioned just over the wheel,
encased by this little ole seat.
I sit there all prim,
but I felt pretty grim
Cos ma legs ud go numb ta ma feet.

Mum ud go like the clappers on thut,
an would sing as she rode me along.
Loves divine an
You are my sunshine
Seemed to be mother's favourite songs.

Now goin ta school wus orite
as the roads were downhill, as they say
so ta my great delight
I could see clear n bright
for almost all a the way.

Now comun back wus a new story.
The hills they did slow up har pace.
She'd stand up n push hard on the pedals
but guess whut wus right in my face?

Now at this point I couldn't do nothun,
Couldn't move or git rid a the sight.
I just sit there still,
till were over the hill.
Then it all went from black back ta white.

MY POPGUN

My dad made me a popgun,
the best one I did see.
Thut dint corst him a penny
but thut meant the world ta me.

He used Elder from the hedges
thut wus ta be the barrel part.
He took thut up the shud
an he made thut look right smart.

He bored the core out a the middle
an made the hole just so,
when the acorn was pushed in
thut hed room ta pop n go.

Then he found a hard ole stick
an in the barrel, made ut fit.
He left a round bit for the handle
So I could hold ma grip with it.

With thut done I ran to the fields,
got Acorns by the score.
I popped them out thut gun
from 10.o.Clock, till half past four.

A little toy a lot a love
an ire just gotta say,
"Why can't they make popguns,
with a lotta love today"?

THE WEEDS ULL BE BACK

Ma garden look sa lovely now
thut wus a mess afore
um so glad now ire cleared ut up
an can't see the weeds no more.

They grew all round ma Tulips
an round the bottom a ma tree
till I cut em orf ma trellus
I dint know I hed sweet Pea.

Thut wont stay like thut forever
you wont know where ire bin
cos in two days time I bet ya life
Thull orl be back agin.

Ma knees are wet n mucky
Ire got a blister fit ta pop
now ull stop n hev a cuppa tea
cos um feelun fit... ta drop.

I like the winter best
Cos there's one thing you can claim
an thus after the snow has fallen
all our gardens look the same.

QUOTE!

I was with my father-in-law Frank in his
garden one spring time when the ole chap
over the way came out a his house.........

"blast me thus a warm one today boy",
he said to Frank,

to which Frank replied, " yis , but you know
what they say. "don't cast ya clout till May
is out".

"no", he answered,
"n as my poor ole mother used ta say.

" you shount tearke nuthun orf".

COLLECTUN ACORNS FOR PIGS

I remember the galvanised pail
thut I used ta carry around
I'd fill ut right up wi acorns
they'd fell orf the trees ta the ground.

On a Saturday I'd go out huntun
under gret big ole heavy oak trees
Just ta fill the pail up ta the brim
I'd go home wi mud up ta ma knees.

I loved the fresh air n the peace
I dint care about work n no play
Just ta fill the pail wus an achievement
I dint care if thut took me all day.

The smell a damp grass n the ditches
the wildlife n their funny habits
An I'd allus go home wi some hogweed
fa ma dad ta feed ta ma rabbits.

The man up the rood hed the acorns
his little pigs loved em a rummun.
An while he paid me ta gorn git em
them ole acorns well they kept a cummun.

WE SOLD PAPERWEIGHTS

My friend Joss was wuss than me
she'd giggle all day long.
Sometimes she'd laugh sa much
we'd both on us git wrong.

We'd orften think a good ideas
ta mearke some pocket money
an the things thut we got up to
were sometimes really funny.

We once sold stones as paperweights
we chose an painted em
we took the paint from har dads shud
an they really looked a gem.

We laid a tearble by the roodside
an we thought they'd sell sa fast.
We put em for a penny each
as the local folk walked past.

We thought we'd mearke a fortune
but in truth we mearde 2p.
But did we ? I bought one from har
an she bought one orf me.

WINKLES ORF THE MARKET

My sisters orften brought em home
an blast they stunk an all.
Um talkun about them winkles
from the Norwich Market stall.

The two gals orften sat there
an what I sight I saw.
Both on em eatun winkles
on the step outside the door.

Each on em wi a little pin
would pick the black bit out
an stick it on their cheeks
or just below their snout.

They thought thut they looked lovely
but ire gotta tell ya what,
they needed more than winkles
ta give them a beauty spot.

I used ta stand n watch,
What ever were they thinkun?
As a tomboy, even I knew
no one ud want em…spots n stinkun.

But the trend that went wi fashion
An times they are a changun
an I reckon they thought at the time
thut Tina, she's a strangun.

An they hint made up too badly
they're done well n got nice plearces.
But they never got their husbands
when they hed winkles on their fearces.

FEEDUN THE PIGS

Ole Sally pig a gruntun
an har littluns squeakun back
an my dad a tippun meal
ta mix wi water from a sack.

She hed har little young uns
an I thought thut thut won't fare
dad won't let me coax em
while ole Sally stood sa near

He say, "gal don't you go near em,
till ole Sally hev har meal,
then ull git har trorf outer the way
then you ken hev a feel".

He reckoned she might tun on me
then maybe ull git bit.
Or she'd push me over wi har snout
an land me in the... muck.

So dad ud gather up the grub
tearter peel an all,
he'd feed thut ta ole Sally
up the corner near the wall.

I'd stroke them little Piglets
they felt sorft n warm n silky,
but if I got close ta cuddle em
they dint half smell bloomun stinky.

I remember thut ole Sty as if
I stood in there today,
wi them pigs a chowun round me
cos um plonked right in the way.

We'd clean the Sty out orften,
wi ma wellys I would be
I'd stink like that ole Pig Sty
but thut dint bother me.

Me n dad n Sally pig
an you could not mistearke,
the straw, the muck, the noise, the grub
Wut a picture thut ud mearke.

OLD WYMONDHAM SALE YARD

On a Friday me n mum n dad
If the weather didn't fail
We'd climb inta our Ford Anglia
an head orf ta Wymondham Sale.

The old yard wus situated
as you turned inta the town,
but later moved to Station Lane
an the ole buildings got knocked down.

I loved thut little Auction yard
so quaint an quite ornate,
an I'd feel so excited
as we drove in through the gate.

The hustle n bustle the hoards a stuff
the people we all knew.
A great day out n we hed a laugh
so much ta see n do.

There'd be rabbits in the hutches
some wi younguns some were old
an Dad he liked ta wait n see
what they made when they got sold.

There'd be chickens in the boxes
Scrappun corn under their legs
An the bidders lookun under em
Ta see if they had eggs.

There'd be loads a household goods
Made in rows along the ground.
There'd be boxes filled wi nuthun
but we'd still walk round n round.

Inside the hall ud be the produce
Greens, spuds, an all the rest,
an Mum ud say the furniture in there
Wus all the best.

The ice-cream cart would make a mint
thut was just from me
An mum n dad would buy a roll
an have a cuppa tea.

The dusty hall, uneven ground
the farmers welly boots
The woodbine ash an bacca
Oh! the smell a peoples coats.

I love ta reminisce
memories are all ire got
an if the same come round agin
I'd be there like a shot.

MUM N DAD AT HEMSBY

We asked em both on holiday
they were chuffed as they could be
So orf we went ta Hemsby
Boy David, them n me.

We'd booked a little chalet
wi lino wall ta wall
an thut hed all amenities
a cooker, fridge an all.

Outside there wus a bit a grass
thut housed a linen line.
For a week both on em just relaxed
me n David, we were fine.

They went on the amusements
an in the bingo halls,
But mother she couldn't keep away
from them there penny falls.

She'd saved up all har coppers
an afore we went she say,
"I love them penny platforms
on them ull spend all day".

They were very late fa tea one night
I sent David out ta find em
they come back later safe n sound
wi David right behind em.

I pretended then ta tell em orf
" cum you on, ire cooked ya meal".
Mum say."ire warmed your tea up in the past,
I know just how ya feel!"

One day me n boy David
done some washun out ba hand
an we left mum n dad back there
while we walked acrorss the sand.

When we got back, well what a sight
My mum laid on the bed
an dads asleep out in the sun
Wi mums clean knickers on his head.

Afore they woke, our cameras out
N what a funny shot
The funny, most relaxun scenes
an the ones we're least forgot.

Thut was such a funny holiday
we laughed the whole week through
an mum n dad were so relaxed
that they enjoyed ut too.

THE GARDEN COMPETITION

He loved his country garden
his carrots, spuds an all
an the gardners competition
today in the village Hall.

He washed n cleaned his carrots
they layed out in a line
all shiny, bright, n orange
an the tops looked so divine.

His cabbage clean n leafy
all green n round n hard
put in a big brown cardboard box
at the bottom of the yard.

But his spuds, now let me tell ya
this story made me cry
cos he dug his best n washed em
and they laid outside ta dry.

So imagine when the time had come
to gather up his ware
and he realised half his spuds had gone
just a few on em laid there.

Now, this chap he had a little Dawg
who'd dig round in the mud.
He dint like green n leafy plants
but was partial to a spud.

Well he looked around his garden
for where the spuds had gone
then he saw his little dawg
an what he was chompun on.

Blast me he let a hollar
his missus ran n met im
She say ,"wus wrong wi you, ya silly sod?"
he say, "the dawg a gone n et um".

Well his missus kep a laughun
but he wus bloomun roar
but he got his fork outa the shud
an went n dug some more.

An when he'd laid em out n done
they looked lovely in a row,
an blast me at the village hall
If he dint win the show.

Well done Brian..!

COME YOU WI ME

I knew a young boy he wus handsome
But I was orl proper n good
An I say,"I cant go wi you bor
N ma sister live just down the rood".

He arsked ta tearke holda ma hand
N I said yis I thought thut he could
I said,"don't you dare go any futher
Cos ma sister's jus there down this rood.

So we walked hand in hand a fare way
I hid under ma anorack hood
He say,"I love you"
I say, "blast thut ont do
Wi ma sister there just down the rood.

So we're walkun along the ole path
He leaned over I knew thut he would
He gi me a kiss
I say,"bor thus like this"
Ma sisters just there down the rood.

But thut kiss thut felt sorta orite
An I hint hed a kiss afore hedda
So I say,"thus no good
Wi har just down the rood"
This go back n go over the medda.

MA SISTERS "LUCKY" RABBIT

This story my sister told me
of a poor little rabbut she had.
As soon as she saw ut she knew
she loved ut and so she asked dad,

"Oh please can I hev thut there bunny
thus the tiniest thing I did see,
I promise ull care fa him proper
Oh please will ya give him ta me"?

Well dad looked and on closer inspection
said, "thut bloomun rabbut look queer."
He saw that thut dint hev a tail
an only a half a one ear.

To her thut dint make any diffrence.
She said she still wanted him so,
the rabbut was hers n called Bobby
Although later found HE was a Doe.

She pushed him around in a pram.
She brushed him when he got all mucky.
Such a sweet dear
No tail n one ear
Thut rabbuts nearme shudda bin,"Lucky"

(Well done Chrissy)

JACK VALENTINE

I'd hear a tap upon ma door
I'd run ta see who's there
Instead a little parcel
ud on this day appear.

My mum knew he was comun
My dad he'd disappear
I dint know what Jack looked like
an I dint really care.

He'd leave me sweets an crayons
sometimes a little book.
An my Dad ud come in later
say he'd come ta hev a look.

He never called on orl ma friends
but allus come ta mine
On February 14th
My own Jack Valentine.

THE BAKER

The bearker saw the villages
he'd tap upon the door.
Wi a gret ole wicker basket
on his arm, filled ta the core.

There'd be bread n cearkes n biscuits
all from this little man.
An he'd hev some sweets in boxes
but he'd keep them in the van.

Mum ud buy some biscuits
she'd git gingerbreads fa me
an we all liked thick ole shortbreads
so we could donk em in our tea.

Thut wus fun ta see the bearker
wi his basket an his way
Of heven nothun thut ya want
but ya bought ut anyway.

MOTHERS DAY

Mothers day, a day of thanks
a day fa mums ta rest.
Ta let ya mother know
thut ta you she is the best.

A day when thoughts can wander
When a mother int forgot
Whether still thut they're here with us
or indeed like mine they're not.

A mother can be funny
when ya think of wut they say,
when you're playun in the garden
an they shout across the way,

"Now git you orf thut tree branch
thus dangerous yull see
an if ya fall n break ya leg
well don't you run ta me."

Another one my mum ud say
an quite orften id get flack
is" mearke sure ya got ya vest on gal
yull git cold in ya back"

Now ta you this might sound normal
she worried, but I mean
I did feel quite embarrassed
cos I hed just turned eighteen.

She'd allus be a singun
In the kitchen, on the loo,
I'd tut n raise ma eyebrows
but now I find I do ut too.

Ma mother wus so clever
She'd cook n sew fa days
I arnt the best cook in the world
ire got ma Fathers ways.

My mum wus kind an lovun
an nothun wus a chore.
She enjoyed har home an family
an dint ask fa nothun more.

So if ya feel like me
thut you hev the perfect mother,
Then tearke the time ta tell har thanks
an thut ya really love her.

FATHERS DAY

A father a man ta look up to.
Someone who you know you ken trust,
An mine weren't too bad
I loved me ole dad
he'd mearke me laugh till I near bust.

We'd laugh as we walked wi the dawg,
over fields we'd trearpse at our leisure.
An dad made a habit
a catchun a rabbit,
ta tearke home fa tea fa good measure.

Beside him I'd be in ma wellies
wi ma coat with a zip on the hood.
An my ground I would stand
wi acorns in ma hand
fa ma popgun he'd made out a wood.

The tales he would tell as we wandered
of his days on the farm as a lad,
The jokes they kept cummun
my dad wus a rummun
but he never done nothun too bad.

He taught me to try n stay strong
an ta live by ma means ta git on,
an don't mearke a fuss
cos thut cudda bin wus!
An ta keep out where I don't belong.

He taught me ta mearke do n mend
he would tell me "don't borra yit lend,
an never be shy
To be happy or cry"
My dear dad, my hero my friend.

MY NANNY AND THE SHILLUNS

Each time she come ta our house
by har side I would stand.
No one ud see
when she give me
thut shillun in ma hand.

"Don't ya tell ya Granddad
ire give ya all thut money"
my Nanny said
shakin har head
I thought thut wus really funny.

Cos as they both went out the door
by my Granddad I would stay
An in my hand
A shillun ud land
An he'd turn ta me an say,

"Now don't ya tell ya Nanny
Ire give ya thut cos she
might be short
on food she're bought
an might want thut orf me".

So by keepun this from both on em
my money thut did grow.
A lovely job.
I got two bob.
If they knew, ull never know.

NANNY THE CHIMNEY SWEEP

Of course thut weren't har real job
But she did it really good.
She wus a lovely leardy
Allus helped out where she could.

She hed many kids ta cope with
Hed no time ta laze n sleep.
The locals orften called on har
ta go round n chimney sweep.

My mum told me a story
of one day while Nan wus sweepun
A leardy ran round to the house
hysterical an weepun

"Oh please come round ta our house
my daughters havun a baby"
My nan washed an dried har hands
an went orf ta help the leardy.

Nan helped har daughter ta give birth
a lovely child wus born,
then nanny hed no more ta do
she said,"well um now gorn".

So back ta work she got
with har brushes up the flue,
an finished orf thut job an all
I don't know how di you?

THE FISHUN MATCH

I sit here by the fishun lake
eyes squintun from the sun.
Everyone's caught fishes
n up ta now I hint caught none.

Around me they're so busy
I stare at them n frown
Cos my float thut sit there motionless
thut don't go up yit down.

Ire tried sweetcorn on a fourteen hook
n catfood on a twelve
Ire put things around ma hook
from all the plearces I can delve.

Ire sit n stared n counted
an thought "ull give ut up ta ten
then if by then ma float hint moved
I shant come here argen".

But I still sit by the water
an I must look like a fool
Cos I hint moved for ages
theres a bird sat on ma pole.

I give a little subtle shake
N the birdy fly away
I reckon thus like me ya know
thus hed enough today.

I can't believe ire sit here
N I hint hed a bite
I reckon them ole fish they say
"Well gal, sarve ya right".

I ship in very quietly
undecided whut ta do
I think ull try some maggots
so I hook on just a few.

I put ma pole back in the water
Ma maggots pink n squigley
but they soon fall orf ma hook
cos they're lively fat n wrigley.

I git so fed up I can't go on
I ship in n pack ma stuff.
I know ire bin defeated
So orf I go home in a huff.

IR'E LORST MA HAT

Where's ma bloomun hat gone?
Wherever did thut go?
I hed thut on
ta talk ta John
I wus cold from hid ta toe.

Oh blimey where'd I put ut?
Ire gotta wear thut out
The weathers rough
N thus bad enough
wi the cold around ya snout.

I laid ut on the sideboard
Now where could thut a gone
I come in fa tea
Ut half past three
N I know I hed thut on.

I allus try ta put ut
so I know where that'll be
N I bet my life
thut my dear wife
ha cleared up arter me.

I wish she'd leave ma things alone
Thas har! No need ta prove ut
Thus such a shame
there're all the same
A wifes just gotta move ut.

MY WELLY BOOTS

You all need welly boots
thar the best boots you ken git.
I hint found no other boots
as good as Wellys yit

I wear mine up the garden
they're comfortable n good
an I wear em very orften
when um walkun up the rood.

They're easy ta pull on.
They don't hut ya feet.
The rubbers good n flexable.
The comforts hard ta beat.

So when you're next in Norwich
an you want suffun smart n dashun,
git you a pair a Welly boots
they're never out a fashion.

THUS THE NIGHT AFORE CHRISTMAS

Thus the night afore Christmas
an I sit in ma chair
Dint want ta go pubbin
I'd rather be here.

I stare round ma room
an what do I see?
A festive commotion
crearted by me.

Ma trimmuns look lovely
an um so glad a thut
till I see ma poor Fairy
wi a tree up har skut.

But where else do ya putta
thus a Fairies real plearce
an she's allus got
a rum smile on har fearce.

Ma presents all lay there
Ire shook em n sin em
Jus one night ta go
an ull find out wus in em.

Ire got nuts in ma dishes
an bearsuns ta fill
an fruit on the tearble
though no one is ill.

Ma husbands a rummun
he sit here a squarkun
he's glad um a writun
thut stop me from talkun.

Um ahid wi me bearkun
but thus nothun new
So fust thing tomorra
theres nothun ta do.

Ma sprouts n ma parsnips
Ire left out in water
an he stuff the Tarkey
he don't think I oughta.

Thus bin a rum week
leadun up ta taday
We're bin rushen about
givin presents away.

'Best ta give than receive'
are words often said
but thus nice ta hev suffun
on the end a ya bed.

Be it big or small
oval or square
Um happy wi suffun
just ta show me ya care.

I don't like ta be greedy
thut send ma heart sinkun.
Thus the thought thut count
'So **I sit here thinkun'.**

I soon better git ready
ta go orf ta ma bed,
Do ull meet the ole man
all dressed up in red.

Then wi ma hid on ma pilla
ull take time ta remember
The Birth in the Stable
On 25th December.

MY NORFOLK UPBRINGUN

A little country Bungalow
is where I wus born n raised.
Mum n dad had nine a us
They were the good ole days.

Um Tina, um the youngest
I don't do girlie things like cook
I'd rather be out fishun
Mum said I orta bin a blook.

I learnt ta drive a tractor
I loved thut every bit.
Id pull ma father on the trailer
While he forked orf the chicken..Muck.

We grew our cabbages n spuds
an carrots by the score
I loved the tearst a them
They just arnt the searme na more.

Our ole tin bath ud hang outside
an Fridays arter nosh
We'd hev thut ole bath indoors
an all on us hed a wash.

Mum used ta git ma clothes
From the Army n Navy store
You don't see gals at school
Dressed as soldiers anymore.

You know I love ta reminisce
Our mum n dad were funny
They give us many laughs n love
Ya can't buy thut wi money.

THE LAST ONE IN THE BOOK.

Well here I am the last poem
Um stuck here in this book.
An if ya hint book one
Well thus worth heven a look.

Thus called I SIT HERE THINKUN
On the front, well you'll see me
Oh! An don't forget now
Ire got a first C.D.

I do hope you enjoy ma poems
Of my childhood they are true
Um proud a where I come from
Um Norfolk through n through.

I have been on the radio
On a sundy after two
Wi the lovely Maggie Secker
On Radio Norfolks "Maggies Brew".